MW01537233

PROPERTY OF

Made in the USA
Las Vegas, NV
16 July 2023

74850022R00057